T0128417

'ACT LIKE A CHILD'! THINK LIKE A MATURE CHRISTIAN

MURWEEN ROSE

authorHOUSE

AuthorHouse™
1663 Liberty Drive
Bloomington, IN 47403
www.authorhouse.com
Phone: 833-262-8899

Published by AuthorHouse 03/26/2024

ISBN: 978-1-7283-1480-8 (sc)
ISBN: 978-1-7283-1491-4 (e)

Library of Congress Control Number: 2019907199

Print information available on the last page.

Any people depicted in stock imagery provided by Getty Images are models, and such images are being used for illustrative purposes only. Certain stock imagery © Getty Images.

This book is printed on acid-free paper.

Because of the dynamic nature of the Internet, any web addresses or links contained in this book may have changed since publication and may no longer be valid. The views expressed in this work are solely those of the author and do not necessarily reflect the views of the publisher, and the publisher hereby disclaims any responsibility for them.

Scripture quotations marked KJV are from the Holy Bible, King James Version (Authorized Version). First published in 1611. Quoted from the KJV Classic Reference Bible, Copyright © 1983 by The Zondervan Corporation.

Brethren, do not be children in understanding; however, in malice be babes, but in understanding be mature. (1Cor.14:20) NKJV

...A Practical Devotion   nuggets

The Ultimate Guide for Good Christian Living

CONTENTS

ACKNOWLEDGEMENTS

To my Heavenly Father who gave me the inspirations and strength to write this book.

To my immediate family who exercises their patience, support and encouragements to me in completing this devotional guide.

Special thanks to my editing pal Latona who offered her support in reading my book and offer her expertise.

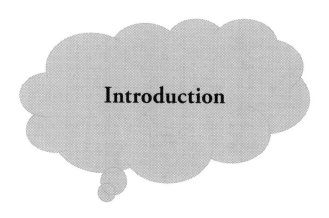

Introduction

There is no doubt that Christians in today's world do love the Lord and are trying to live for the Lord by doing His will. The concern though, through observation and experiences, is that Christians do face various challenges to be the light bearers as God would want them to be.

I chose to write this book as a form of devotion and reflection for all Christians including myself to help in developing and maintaining the right attitude and behaviors that really depict holiness. As one who has various experiences in the counseling environment, I am well aware that behaviors are developed from one stage to another. In the stages of Child Development, a child goes through distinct periods of development as they grow from infancy to young adulthood.

The different topics within this book provide some simple but profound tips that can help Christians to grow as a child of the Heavenly King.

The book title was inspired through a celebrity whom I admire; he wrote a book for his daughters to help them to understand how to think in regards to relationships. As a result, something rested in my spirit. Then immediately I thought, 'what a great blessing it would have been for Christians to act like a child in their behaviors, yet think like a mature Christian in their actions'.

The book is divided into two sections; nuggets and reflections. There are twenty nuggets in the book. They are designed to teach and guide Christians to be humble as a child but mature in their thinking. These nuggets are embedded with the bible verses that are tailored to guide and teach believers on various life challenges or circumstances.

The second section is about reflection. Reflection in its simplest form is the process by which an individual analyze and make judgments about what had happened. Hence, reflection plays a crucial role in a Christian spiritual growth. The reflections are designed in quizzes, questions and bible verses.

Christians are encouraged to keep on living for the Lord in a meaningful way with the aim of entering into eternal life and not just passing through a church with an alternate motive.

Dedication

This book is dedicated to my beloved mother Mable Boothe -Perry (deceased) who was a very good example of how a mature Christian should behave in living for the Lord. My mother was a woman of God who lived her life through demonstrating the appropriate behaviors that portray a child of God. There were times my siblings and I would marvel about her reactions to things that we thought would have made her sad or upset. However, in a very natural and genuine way, she would respond just like a child of the King. Therefore, as a child of God, we should be so in-tune with Him at all times so that our daily lives will say "Yes Lord to your will and to your way".

To be able to act like a child of God and think like a mature Christian is to study the words of the Lord daily.

Nugget # 1: Key Bible Verses
for Christian Reading

Acting like a mature Christian signified one whose characteristics, words, dispositions, and actions emulates the character of Jesus Christ. It is also about demonstrating faith, knowledge of God from His Word, perseverance through hardships, imitating Christ, behaving wisely, developing mutual affection for believers and for the Church, and having compassion for souls.

- When I was a child, I spake as a child, I understood as a child, I thought as a child: but when I became a man, I put away childish things. 1 Corinthians' 13-11
- Brethren, be not children in understanding: howbeit in malice be ye children, but in understanding be men. 1 Corinthians 14:20

1

- I have no greater joy than to hear that my children are walking in the truth. **3John 1-4**
- Little children, let us not love in word or talk but in deed and in truth. **1 John 3:18**

It's impossible to know God without knowing His Word. For a Christian to act like a child and think like a mature Christian, one will have to spend time in the words of God. According to the following scriptures:

- 2 **Timothy** 3:16 All Scripture is given by inspiration of God and is profitable for doctrine, for reproof, for correction, for instruction in righteousness.
- John 15:7 - If ye abide in me, and my words abide in you, ye shall ask what ye will and it shall be done unto you.
- **Romans** 15:4 -For whatsoever things were written aforetime were written for our learning, that we through patience and comfort of the scriptures might have hope.
- **Jeremiah** 15:16 – Thy words were found, and I did eat them; and thy word was unto me the joy and rejoicing of mine heart: for I am called by thy name, O Lord God of hosts.
  - **Matthew 5:16**- Let your light so shine before men, that they may see your good works, and glorify your Father which is in heaven.
  - **Matthew 7:16** – Ye shall know them by their fruits. Do men gather grapes of thorns, or figs of thistles?

- **John 13:35** - By this everyone will know that you are my disciples, if you love one another. When we truly love God, we will have the desire to behave like a child of the King in a mature way.

> When an individual is in that child-like space, it is likely that the behavior will be more genuine and transparent

Act like a child, think like a mature Christian

Nugget # 2: Who is a child of God?

There are multiple schools of thoughts which generically defines who is a child of God. **St John 1-12**-states that, But as many as received him, to them gave he the power to become the sons of God, [even] to them that believe on his name. Therefore it would be safe to say that believing on the Lord Jesus Christ is one of the first steps in starting the Christian process to be called a child of God. Galatians 3-26 For ye are all the children of God by faith in Christ Jesus.

Someone in a conversation stated some time ago, that when the Bible speaks about Christians having the heart of a child, the Bible was not talking about children of today's generation. When asked why, the response was, "These children are unruly from the toddler stage, as they are hitting back and frowning". While there may be some truth in this observation, a child in most cases is innocent and holds no grudge.

This means that a Christian that has a mature attitude will know that he or she has the power through Jesus Christ to become the child God wants him/her to be through faith.

As humans, we all can testify that we were born in sin and shape in iniquity but God is his infinite love allowed Jesus to die so that we can obtain mercy.

A child of God should recognize that God in His infinite love extends mercy even when there are some pain involved. The reason for this is that even though you may have to pray and fast to overcome, God allows things to happen sometimes to help Christian to become more mature children. Romans 8:28 clearly states that all things work together for good to them that love God, to them who are the called according to his purpose.

A child of God should have this verse as a guide post. Personally, I learnt this verse later in my Christian walk, (of which I had some regrets that I did not know it before). Therefore, it is of paramount importance for a child of the King to know that God has a reason and a purpose for everything in his or her life.

A child of God should:

1. be aware that as they live in the world; working, caring, serving, having fun, witnessing, they should not adapt to the worldly pleasures. In Romans 12:2 Paul outlines – *'And be not conformed to this world: but be ye transformed by the renewing of your mind that ye may prove what is good, and acceptable, and perfect, will of God'*.
2. not conformed to the world, look like the world, dress like the world or behave like the world. This is a loaded statement but we were instructed to be different as what is outlined in 2 Cor. 6:17 & 18.

3. not think themselves higher than others, as we are one in Christ our Lord.

Gentleness

Kindness

Love

Patience

Self-Control

Faithfulness

Generosity

Joy

Peace

This Fruit is Always in Season

The fruit of the spirit can blossom in grace when we read the words of the Lord daily and live them out in our lives. !!

Act like a child, think like a mature Christian

Nuggets # 3: The characteristics of a mature Christian

A childlike attitude can be described as behaviors that demonstrate humility and grace. This does not mean that one must be treated or act as a child but rather taking on the characteristics of the Lord Jesus Christ. As Christians we must strive to become like Christ by eradicating sin from our lives and replacing it with Godly living. In doing so, we will begin to achieve spiritual maturity. According to Galatians 5:22-23, the fruits of the Spirit are love, joy, peace, longsuffering, gentleness, goodness, faith, meekness, temperance: against such there is no law.

Some important traits of a child of God behaviors are:

- ➤ **Love**- A child will love even when there maybe a misunderstanding. Love chooses to set aside one's own preferences, desires, and sometimes even needs to put the other person first. (Luke 6:35 & 1 Cor. 13)
- ➤ **Joy**- The joy of the Lord is my strength." -Nehemiah 8:10

"A child of God should show forth the joy of the Lord in good times and bad times.

➢ **Peace**- Jesus said, "Blessed are the peacemakers: for they shall be called the children of God" (matt 5:9). A child of God should first be at peace with themselves and be prepared at all times for the various experiences that will call for them to show peace to all or be at peace with your neighbors.

➢ **Longsuffering**- Rejoicing in hope; patient in tribulation; continuing instant in prayer, Romans 12:12. Longsuffering is said to be a virtue which Christians can develop over a period of time when face with adversity in life."

➢ **Gentleness**- Gentleness is showing the courage to care for others. Be ye kind one to another, tenderhearted, forgiving one another, even as God for Christ's sake hath forgiven you. Ephesians 4:32

➢ **Goodness**- The goodness and unfailing love of the Lord will pursue you all the days of your life. Surely goodness and mercy shall follow me all the days of my life: and I will dwell in the house of the LORD forever.(Psalms 23-6)

➢ **Faith**- But without faith [it is] impossible to please [him]: for he that cometh to God must believe that he is, and [that] he is a rewarder of them that diligently seek him.(Hebrews 11-6) Having faith is recognizing that you have no control, of what will be, and that there is a greater power to see you through.

➢ **Meekness**- Jesus taught a lesson on meekness which is a criteria to inherit the earth (Matt.5-5). To be meek does not suggest you are weak in dealing with matters of concerns but to deal with it with a humble nature. It also suggest that one should be teachable, and patient while going through trials.

➢ **Temperance**- Temperance can be viewed as moderation in thought, word, or action; it comes down to the choices that we make in our lives. And to knowledge temperance; and to temperance patience; and to patience godliness (2 Peter 1-6).

When life challenges becomes difficult to
bear, seek the Lord with all your hearts.

Act like a child, think like a mature Christian

Nugget # 4: Christian responding to daily life challenges-(An Inward Fight)

It's easy to feel hopeful, when life is going well but when life brings trouble and trials, feelings of hopelessness can easily creep in.

Life sometimes comes with uncomfortable experiences which sometimes cause distress to the believers' heart. But as a child of God it is important to note the end result, which is to take God at His words in every situation. James 1:2-3 states, 'My brethren, count it all joy when ye fall into divers temptations; knowing this, that the trying of your faith worketh patience'.

Christians live in a world of crisis, where they will be disappointments, trouble, hard times, financial deprivations, sicknesses, death, accidents and all other types of life challenges. Any of these issues can face Christians at any time. It is important to note that as mature believer, we will never go through any of these experiences alone. The word of God provides instructions, directions, consolations, and advice as to how to navigate the way to cope with such situations.

There may be times when the refrigerator will be empty;

the bank account is low or empty, bills to be paid, health problems, your spouse may walk out on you or may not be treating you well, loss of a loved one and loss of a job. All of these experiences does give a sense of gloom but always go back to the words of God for solace, hope and comfort. The songwriter lost all, yet he found solace in the Lord and he wrote the hymn; "It is well with my Soul".

The LORD is nigh unto them that are of a broken heart; and saveth such as be of a contrite spirit (Ps. 34-18) and Ps, 46-1 reminds us that God is our refuge and strength, a very present help in trouble. Responding to life's challenges with the words of God allows one to develop more faith and confident in the Creator. He is well aware of your situations just keep on trusting and believing and He will help you to respond to life's situations like a mature child of God.

God sometimes allow for the child of God to experience troublesome times as a learning experience which can help the child of God to develop more trust in a deeper way in him.

Be careful how we complain when life presents challenges as they sometimes comes to test and build character

Kindness is free take it wherever you go and share it!!

Act like a child, think like a mature Christian

Nugget # 5: Christians dealing with conflicts with others in a Christ-like way (An outward Fight)

For a Christian to act like a child indicates one having a childlike attitude and a childlike behavior when it comes to righteousness. Every Christian faces myriad of problems and obstacles in their lives. However, how one deal with those situations will differentiate a mature Christian from one that is not. In Matt 18: 1-4, Jesus used a child to illustrate to His disciples that they are not be childish in their behaviour, arguing over trivial issues, but rather childlike, with humility and sincere hearts. Hence, when you are confronted with an issue/problem, be mature in the way you handle the situation and your response should be embedded in the words of the Lord, for example:

- ✓ Take a moment for yourself as needed and do some introspection instead of lashing out (Proverbs 4-15)
- ✓ Pray about the issue at hand – Psalm 34-4
- ✓ Engage in a dialogue not a quarrel (proverbs 15-1)

- ✓ Acknowledge what went wrong
- ✓ Make amend sooner rather than later
- ✓ Focus on reconciliation and forgive

Whenever you feel like rolling your fist, stamping your feet, point up a close finger, raise a hand or behave unseemly, just refer to the question Paul asks in Romans 8:35-39 Who shall separate us from the love of Christ? Shall tribulation, or distress, or persecution, or famine, or nakedness, or peril, or sword?

As it is written, For thy sake we are killed all the day long; we are accounted as sheep for the slaughter. Nay, in all these things we are more than conquerors through him that loved us. For I am persuaded, that neither death, nor life, nor angels, nor principalities, nor powers, nor things present, nor things to come, nor height, nor depth, nor any other creature, shall be able to separate us from the love of God, which is in Christ Jesus our Lord

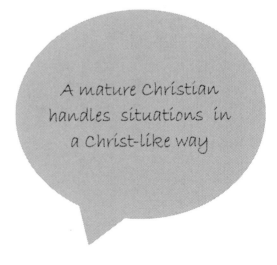

A mature Christian
handles situations in
a Christ-like way

Act like a child, think like a mature Christian

Nugget # 6: A mature Christian epitomizes Christ.

It is expected that individuals who are Christ-like should behave in a way that depicts righteousness and exemplifies Christ. This goes for both male and female as the Lord sees both gender as His children.

Paul said in Galatians 3:28 *"There is neither Jew nor Greek, there is neither bond nor free, there is neither male nor female: for ye are all one in Christ Jesus. Children of God should be light bearers at home, on the job, in the community and in the larger society"*.

➢ A mature Christian knows how to treat each other in a Godly way. They are aware of the 'beam in their eyes before acknowledging the beam in others eyes.

➢ Mature Christians should be mindful of their words in regards to when to share their thoughts and when it may not be okay to do so. This can only be possible when we walk in the spirit.

> ➤ Mature Christians learn to cope with situations and pray at all times, even when they don't understand the reasons why they are going through it. The key factor here is making sure the words of God are not compromise in their actions.

> ➤ Mature Christians when hurt about life issues, should not have an anger tantrum; instead, whenever the feeling of anger overwhelm them, they should talk about the problem with grace and love.

> ➤ Mature Christians should not go on social media to vent about an issue to convey a message directly or indirectly to another believer, a friend or a minister. There are other ways to talk about matters in a Godly manner.

> ➤ Mature Christians should learn how to cope with neighbors, church family, friends, in-laws when they do us wrong. This can only be a success if believers rely fully on God who will give the strength to cope in those moments.

I am well aware of what hurting looks like. I am also aware that it can allow an individual to vent the wrong way that bring some satisfaction to the mind. But whatever the situation is, it should be always dealt with in a Godly manner. The lesson I learn from that experience was that there are verses in the Bible that can help us to respond and solve the problems at hand.

Perfect love cast out all fears

Act like a child, think like a mature Christian

Nugget # 7: Christians winning souls for the Kingdom

One of the greatest joys that any Christians can have is the joy of leading someone to Christ. The songwriter asked an important question, 'Will there be any star! Any star on my crown?' A star here could be viewed as winning souls. As a result, accumulating stars on your crown is a benefit. Although we know that it is not a literal crown with stars, every child of God should be thinking maturely in winning souls for the kingdom of God. When Jesus was leaving earth, He commissioned his disciples to teach all nation to observe all things whatsoever He have commanded them (Matt. 28: 18-20). Therefore, every child of God is called upon to win souls for the kingdom of God. Jesus being our example says follow me, and I will make you fishers of men. (Matthew 4:19).

It is quite evident that not every believer will be an evangelist by title or very skilled in sharing the gospel of Christ but we can all share with others the good news that **Jesus loves them and that he died on that old rugged cross for the redemption of our sin (Romans 12:6-8 & 1 Peter 4:10).** Another simple way of winning souls for Christ is to be an example in words and actions as what is outlined by Jesus in Matt. 5:16, *"Let your light so shine before men that they may see your good work and led to glorified God who art in heaven."*

Therefore, to win soul, it is not recommended to just tell individuals about your church, the day you worship or that they are going to hell if they don't accept Jesus. Instead, gently invite them to meet Jesus. *He that <u>winneth</u> souls is wise."* -Proverbs 11:30

The life Christians live should speak volume to those around them. Be careful what we say and what we do. Very important, mature Christians should not speak loudly or quarrel to get the attention of neighbors to wonder what may be going on in the home of a Christian among spouses or children.

The story was told of an unsaved person having a conversation with a Christian and he observed the Christian using slangs for example (damn) and for him he believes that a Christian should not use certain types of colloquial language. The lesson here for Christians is that even though we are aware that we are not perfect and we do make mistakes we need to bear in mind that the world is looking on.

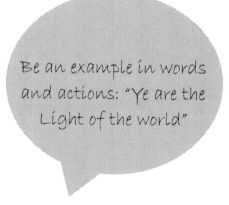

Be an example in words and actions: "Ye are the Light of the world"

Winning souls for Christ should be one of the Christian greatest pleasures. Reach out to someone today!

Nugget # 8: Christians praying
with a child-like heart

The Lord left on record an example of how one should pray to the Father. Jesus always addresses his father when praying by saying "Our Father who art in Heaven, hallowed be thy name". The key factor for Christians is to always acknowledge the divine authority of the Lord first and to pray sincerely and earnestly.

The story was told of two individuals in the Bible who went to the temple to pray. One prayed with a humble and child-like heart by asking the Lord to have mercy on him as a sinner while the other prayed by exalting himself stating his good works and that he was happy that he was not like the other (Luke 18:10-14). Mature Christians should pray sincerely acknowledging the Lord as the Savior of their lives with a contrite and honest heart bearing in mind that the Lord knows the hearts of mankind. He cannot be fooled at any time.

Christians should not only pray for themselves and their families but prayers should be extended to neighbors, schools, communities, children, young adults, the government and for those in the hospitals and in prisons. More importantly, let us not forget the unsaved when we pray. Jesus said in John 17:20-21: *"Neither pray I for these alone, but for them also which shall believe on me through their word; That they all may be one; as thou, Father, art in me, and I in thee, that they also may be one in us: that the world may believe that thou hast sent me".*

Other key principles to practice praying with a child-like heart:

1. Pray simple with expectations
2. Pray with a contrite heart
3. Pray with gratitude and thanksgiving
4. Pray and listen to the voice of the Lord

The effectual fervent prayer of a righteous man availeth much

Act like a child, think like a mature Christian

Nuggets # 9: Christians dwelling on the things of God

Living in today's world, Christians do face different types of temptations, trials, and persecutions. Therefore, if one needs to mature spiritually, he/she needs to dwell on the things of Christ by living each day with a strong desire to please the Lord. Phil 4-8 speaks volume to such characteristics; *"Finally, brethren, whatsoever things are true, whatsoever things are honest, whatsoever things are just, whatsoever things are pure, whatsoever things are lovely, whatsoever things are of good report; if there be any virtue, and if there be any praise, think on these things".*

To dwell on things of the Lord is to be renewed in spirit and in mind. Therefore, if anyone is in Christ, he is a new creation. The old has passed away. Behold, the new has come! 2 Corinthians 5:17. To be a new man or a new woman is to behave circumspectly and behave in a way that does not reflect the world.

One benefit that Christians can gain from dwelling on the things of God: Is by having their basic needs met by living through the words of the Lord daily.

For a Christian to be matured spiritually, the basic needs must be met by living according to the words of the Lord. For example:

Food - the bread of life.

Shelter - Coverage

Air - breathe on me breath of life.

Clothing - Clothed in his righteousness'.

1. **FOOD**
   - Fill the soul - **Jeremiah** 15:16 – Thy words were found, and I did eat them
   - Quench your thirst- **John 4:13-14** - Everyone who drinks of this water will thirst again; but whoever drinks of the water that I will give him shall never thirst.
   - Medicine to the flesh- **Proverbs 4:20-22** -For they are life unto those that find them, and health to all their flesh.
2. **SHELTER- Proverbs 18:10**-The name of the LORD is a strong tower; the righteous runs into it and is safe.
3. **AIR- Job 33:4**- The spirit of God hath made me, and the breath of the Almighty hath given me life.
4. **CLOTHING- Rev. 19-8** -And to her was granted that she should be arrayed in fine linen, clean and white: for the fine linen is the righteousness of saints.

Colossians 3:16 says, *"Let the word of Christ dwell in you richly in all wisdom, teaching and admonishing one another with psalms, hymns and spiritual songs, singing with grace in your hearts to God.* "Having such rich indwelling of the word of God will help you to reach spiritual maturity.

Act like a child, think like a mature Christian

Nugget # 10: Christian life at home, work and church.

When one comes to the Lord , his or her life will be under daily scrutiny at home, work, church and in the community at large. Resisting temptations sometimes can be a difficult task for Christians, especially in the workplace and in the community. Romans 12: 2 states, "Do *not be conformed to this world, but be transformed by the renewing of your mind which will help you to discern what is good, pleasing, and lead you to the perfect will of God.*

Christians ought to be aware that in moments of temptations there will be a force to encounter, a force that wants to block out your righteous thinking and may even show you a way out after yielding to temptation. The devil is so cunning and may even tell you to go ahead and do as you pleased as you will be forgiven. When pressured by any form of temptations, the right thing to do is to walk away from the situation at hand. Be mindful of the fight or flight hormone which is release in response to a stressful, exciting, dangerous or threatening situation which further helps the body to either fight or flee. As a child of God when cornered by temptations, praying and praising is highly recommended.

Christians living in a world of sin should walk worthy of the lord by trying to live for him in all aspects of their lives here on earth. Three of those places are home, work and church. Any of these places has the potential to allow believers to need total dependence on God by reading the words of the Lord to be an overcomer. 2 Corinthians'5- 15 states ... And that he died for all, that they which live should not henceforth live unto themselves, but unto him which died for them, and rose again.

It is ironic how Christians seems to forget sometimes that home is their first ministry. Home for the child of God should be peaceful and loving with fair and respectful disagreements, not intense quarrels, and abusive physical and emotional behaviors.

Tips that Christians can use to evaluate the way they live:

Christians at home:

- All behaviors should epitomize the behavior that glorifies God
- Do unto others the things you desire to be done unto you
- Engage the family in prayer and devotions
- Talk with each other
- Plan together when necessary
- For parents, guard your children with the help of the Lord from those who will cause physical, emotional or sexual harm to them.

- Teach them the way of the Lord
- Couples should be an example in words and actions in their homes.

Christians at work:

- Be careful of gossiping
- Be alert of involving in mischief
- Be honest to yourself and with each other
- Work honestly, bearing in mind that whatever you do is unto God.
- Be on time for work.

Christians at church:

Church is a place where individuals should go to learn about the words of the Lord, to worship and adore him. The Christian at church are sinners saved by grace with the desire to grow and develop in the Lord. There are however various types of Christians with multiple intentions, some with faithful hearts, good desires, and the willingness to allow the Lord to order their steps in his words. While others may just settle to be affiliated to a church.

Types of individuals who attend church:

- ☐ Sons and daughters of the Almighty- always willing to serve
- ☐ The member- never late for worship
- ☐ The believer – show readiness for the work of the Lord at all times
- ☐ The worshipper- always ready for worship

- ☐ The Minister- Never forget their bibles
- ☐ The caretaker- very engage with the plans and duty of the church
- ☐ The 'rebellious'- wait for every unguarded moment to attack
- ☐ The gossipers- pay attention to every word and whispers.
- ☐ The joker- Just coming because of.............
- ☐ The sincere- reading the words and making every effort to apply them to his /her life
- • The usher- never late to open the doors

Most of the above titles are very essential for the work of the Lord and in most cases these individuals have the potential and the desire to do great things for the Lord. But it takes a child-like nature to be able to do the will of God in a sincere way. Romans 12-1 reminds us as mature Christians "I beseech you therefore, brethren, by the mercies of God, that ye present your bodies a living sacrifice, holy, acceptable untoGod, which is your reasonable service. Romans 12:2 also informs That ye may prove what is that good, and acceptable, and perfect will of God. Do not be conformed to this world, but be transformed by the renewing of your mind which will help you to discern what is good, pleasing, and lead you to the perfect will of God. It is therefore important for every child of God to be intentional about the reasons for going to church.

Yield not to Temptations, for yielding is sin

Nugget # 11: Christians going through Tribulations

Tribulation can be defined as great suffering and hardships that a Christian may face on the journey of becoming a child of the Heavenly King.

Tribulation comes in various forms sometimes to test the believer faith in God and their identity. Another work that tribulation does is to assess the Christian sense of purpose and their belief systems. James 1- 2-3 states -my brethren, count it all joy when ye fall into divers' temptations; knowing this, that the trying of your faith worketh patience. It is important for Christians to know that trials and tribulations may come to help them to build a deeper relationship with their heavenly father.

Some reasons why we are tested and how we can be an overcomer:

- **To refine us-** In **Isaiah 48:10** God said, "Behold, I have refined thee, but not with silver; I have chosen thee in the furnace of affliction". When we are going through our afflictions, God is indeed getting rid of the dross that covers us so that we can get to the place where He wants us to be. God also said in **Zechariah 13:9** - And I will bring the third part through the fire, and will refine them as silver is refined, and will try them as gold is tried: they shall call on my name, and I will hear them: I will say, It is my people: and they shall say, The LORD is my God.

- **To help us mature or grow-** Many times as Christians we become stagnant in our growth. At times when this happens, God allows trials and tribulations to come our way so that we can start growing again. Paul in **1 Corinthians 10:13** states – *"There hath no temptation taken you but such as is common to man: but God is faithful, who will not suffer you to be tempted above that ye are able; but will with the temptation also make a way to escape, that ye may be able to bear it".* This can be concluded with a statement Peter said in **2 Peter 3:18** – *"But grow in grace, and in the knowledge of our Lord and Saviour Jesus Christ. To him be glory both now and forever. Amen".*

- **To develop our faith-** There are many instances in the Old and New Testaments that our fellow brothers and sisters were tested. They went through various trails. Paul is one such example. He was one of the greatest apostles ever lived, yet he went through various trials (2 Cor. 11:22-33). Nevertheless, after each trial his faith was grown. **James 1:12** states, *"Blessed is the man that endureth* *temptation: for when he is tried, he shall receive the crown of life, which the Lord hath promised to them that love him".*

- **To encourage others by proving to them that we are living witnesses of our Lord Jesus Christ-** One may asked, "Why do good people have to suffer?" The answer to this is that there are situations that Christians will go through that are not for their immediate benefit but it is to develop the character of someone else. **Job 1** states, *"There was a man in the land of Uz, whose name was* Job; and that man was blameless and upright, and one who feared God and shunned evil". In this profound statement we can recognize that Job didn't do anything wrong but God allowed Satan to afflict him because he was the one that was able to withstand those trials. With all that Job went through, the word of God said he did not sin (Job 1:22). As a result of Job's resounding faith, today Christians continue to live by his example.

And we know that all things work together for good to them that love God, to them who are the called according to his purpose. (Rom.8-28) which could mean that the tribulations has a divine purpose. I truly believe that tribulations have both a purpose and a reward. *"But thanks be to God, who gives us the victory through our Lord, Jesus Christ our lord. Bear in mind believers that, the Lord has assured us that no trial will test us beyond what we can bear and that he will also provide a way for us to stand.* 1cor.10-13 affirms us There hath no temptation taken you but such as is common to man: but God is faithful, who will not suffer you to be tempted above that ye are able; but will with the temptation also make a way to escape, that ye may be able to bear it.

Here are three questions that Christians can consider when going through tribulations:

1. How am I responding to my trials and tribulations?
2. How should I respond to tribulations?
3. Am I learning from the experience?

Life can take us places that is filled with troubles and pain sometimes; but be strong in the power of the Lord. He CAN see you through!

Reading the words will help Christians to grow
and blossom in a mature child of the king.

Act like a child, think like a mature Christian

Nugget # 12: Christians growing in the knowledge of the Lord

Growing in the knowledge of the Lord is when believers spend quality time in His words. This is where Christians should search the scriptures and become acquainted with His words and believe His truth and not just what a pastor says.

Psalm 1:2 informs us: *"But his delight is in the law of the Lord, and in His law he meditates day and night"*

When we read and meditate on the words of the Lord, God will allow his holy spirit to guide us is all truth.

2 Timothy 2:15 states: *"Study to shew thyself approved unto God, a workman that needeth not to be ashamed, rightly dividing the word of truth"*.

Human growth and development in counseling can be viewed as a lifelong process as it relates to your physical, behavioral, cognitive, and emotional growth. This process goes from the infant to childhood stage, from childhood stage to adolescence, and from adolescence to adulthood.

Enormous changes take place during these developmental stages. This is similar to Christians developing in the Lord; there should be a change in our behavior and our faith in God as we developed from the time we accepted the Lord and continuing on the journey serving the Lord.

Christians should be eager to study the words and share them with others. Let us adopt the principles of the Bereans believers who "received the word with great eagerness" (Acts 17-10-11).

It is so important for Christians to have an open mind to learn the truth of the words of God and not just what one may believe from a child, or from the church's stance. Hebrews 2:1 reminds us; *"therefore we ought to give the more earnest heed to the things which we have heard, lest at any time we should let them slip".*

Therefore, Christian should at all times strive to get a better understanding of the scriptures which presents the truth of God's love, His will, His commands and His grace. (Acts 18:24-26). No matter who we are, God wants us to grow in the knowledge of his words so that we can be bold to preach, encourage and witness for him. We don't want to be found lacking like the people in **Hosea 4:6:** *"My people are destroyed for lack of knowledge: because thou hast rejected knowledge, I will also reject thee, that thou shalt be no priest to me: seeing thou hast forgotten the law of thy God, I will also forget thy children".*

Mature Christians should apply the same process to maintain and grow their spiritual development. As mature as Paul was, he did not consider himself to have achieved perfection such that he could cease striving to improve. He forgot past achievements and failures and pressed on to accomplish growth. Philippians' 3-14 declares- I press toward the mark for the prize of the high calling of God in Christ Jesus. Let us grow in the grace and knowledge of our Lord and Savior Jesus Christ. 2 Peter 3:18

1 Corinthians 10:12 – "*Therefore let him who thinks he stands take heed lest he fall.* Christians' should never feel as they are so strong that they cannot fall as this would be a false claim. A child of God can only stay strong by reading the words of the Lord meditating, be on guard through fasting and prayers.

- Hebrews 6-1- Therefore leaving the principles of the doctrine of Christ, let us go on unto perfection; not laying again the foundation of repentance from dead works, and of faith toward God.
- Ephesians 4:14, 15 - Be no longer children, but grow up in Christ.
- 2 Thessalonians 1:3 - The Thessalonians grew remarkably in faith.
- In Philippians 1:9 - Paul was concerned about the love of the saints and prayed for their love to abound more and more.
- 1 Peter 2:2 – said that Christians desire the pure milk of the word that they may grow thereby.

When we read the words of the Lord, there should be a visual growth in our behavior. Let us be mindful of the way we use these statements as a defense mechanism not to change and grow:

- This is how I am
- This is how I was born

- I can't do better because it's in my genes
- I don't care
- I just say what comes to my mind
- I am afraid of no one
- I want to tell them a piece of my mind
- I am not bowing to no one.

Many of the problems we face today is a result of us failing to grow through his words. Let us examine ourselves as Christians and ask God to turn on the search light on us (Psalm 139:23-24).

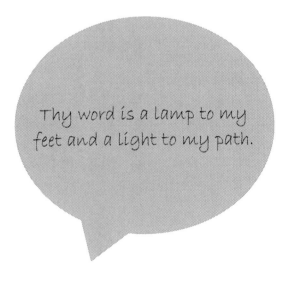

Thy word is a lamp to my feet and a light to my path.

Act like a child, think like a mature Christian

Nugget # 13: Christians managing anger appropriately

Anger can be defined as a strong feeling of displeasure, annoyance, vexation, irritation or hostility. Any of these terms could be used to describe an individual experience when face with challenges along life journey. It is normal to experience anger. At times, anger is the suitable response to the actions of others and sometimes can be necessary for survival. But the key factor here for believers is that they should develop a level of self-control which will assist them when they are tempted to say or do the wrong thing. Believers should also try and refrain from high levels of anger outburst as it does not depict the mature Christian's heart.

The child of God can make the decision to either trust God to be their advocate with the thought that God is bigger than any feelings and he has given Christians the grace to behave in the right way.

Anger can be a serious problem for the believer, Colossians 3:8 states, *"but now you also, put them all aside:*

anger, wrath, malice, slander, and filthy communications from your mouth."

Christians should at all times analyze whether their anger represent a righteous behavior or a sinful one. On more than one occasion, Jesus was not pleased when he encountered unbelief and pretense among worshippers. In John 2:14-17, he drove the people out who were selling in the temple; in Matt 21:12-13 when he over turn the tables of the money changers and in Mark 3:5- when he was watched for doing good healing the man with the withered hand on the Sabbath day. It is a normal reaction that Christians can become angry against evil but it should not over power you to the point of sinning. God warns, be ye angry, and sin not let not the sun go down upon your wrath (Ephesians' 4-26)

At no time should a child of God allow themselves to be out of control, or insulting each other.

Bear in mind though that this is only possible if a believer mind is stayed on God.

From a counseling point of view, one way to deal with anger is by getting in touch with how you feel about an issue and then expressing it. This sometimes allow for an individual to vent how they are feeling about a situation without being judged. Individuals can also use assertive skills to express anger as assertiveness is recommended as a great technique to deal with anger. An assertive person will state what they need in a direct manner while being in control of their emotions in a calm manner.

For every 60 seconds of anger and strife, a believer gave up 1 minute of a calm peace of mind

Nugget # 14: Christians managing false accusation

By one definition, false accusation can be viewed as statements used intentionally for the purpose of deception or to hurt an individual. False accusations can be emotionally charged, but it is crucial to remain calm in your truth. I've had situations in life when hurtful, untrue things were said about me to others which was not easy to bear. The lesson that was learned is that in most cases, people who falsely accuse others or say mean things are often acting from a place of hurt, selfishness, jealousy, bitterness and un-forgiveness. What was helpful though is having a relationship with the Lord and staying in his presence as I was going through.

When you are lied on, always remember that Jesus was falsely accused, but he "held His peace" (Matthew 26-59-63). In order to cope when lied on, it is recommended that the believer take the humbling path; never try too hard to prove your truth. Instead stand by your truth and trust the Lord to make it plain. Your Heavenly father knows it all and He knows your truth! Never allow someone's false words or hurtful actions derail you from fulfilling your God's calling on your life.

Some tips to help:

- When you are lied on, stay calm and seek the Lord in prayer for his guidance.
- Say I did not do that, or I did not say it and hold your peace.
- Assess the problem and pray for directions through the words.
- Have a conversation with the person **if all possible**
- Protect yourself from individuals who continue to lie
- Pray with and for the person if possible
- Forgive the person and move on with your life.

Sometimes the persons who accused you falsely may not want to rectify, apologize or clear your name which can be extremely difficult on your side. But reflect on the fact that God knows you and he knows your heart and your truth so trust him!

Murween Rose

Act like a child, think like a mature Christian

Nugget # 15: Christians managing negative criticism

Christians will experience some form of criticism along the journey to the kingdom of God. The dictionary defines criticism as "an activity of making careful judgments about the good and bad qualities of someone. However, it is most often used to describe negative commentary about something or someone. This action could be viewed as analyzing a person's character. Criticism is however considered to be a normal part of life, but what is essential is the way Christian respond to negative criticisms. As Christians we should therefore rely on the words of the Lord to equip us to deal with the impact that negative criticism can cause.

Another helpful tip is to have a conversation with the person who is observed to be doing the wrong thing. This should be done with grace, love and respect as what is noted in James 5:19-20. The Christian measuring stick should always be the Word of God. Not all criticisms prove true as some critics may just judge a person based on their own perceptions.

As a child of God, be careful not to get bitter when people offend you, Hebrew 12:1 states. Wherefore seeing we also are compassed about with so great a cloud of witnesses, let us lay aside every weight, and the sin which doth so easily beset us, and let us run with patience the race that is set before.

Some other tips that can help:

- Be slow to become angry when others speak evil of you. Remember, God is slow to anger, patient and long-suffering with us all. James 1:19-20
- Listen to what is being said and respond according to Christian principles. (James 1:19) Try not to speak quickly. Take a moment and think about how God would respond to this situation; if you speak too quickly you might speak rashly or in anger.
- Give a gentle response. "A soft answer turns away wrath" (Proverbs 15:1)
- Bear in mind that when Jesus was reviled, he reviled not again; when he suffered, he threatened not; but committed himself to him that judgeth righteously. (1 Peter 2:23).
- Never be too quick to defend yourself as defensiveness could trigger your ego.
- Everyone has blind spots but as a child of God, just remember that the cross makes a difference.

When things become difficult, ask the Lord for wisdom to guide you through the process. (Psalms 32:8). "I will instruct you and teach you in the way you should go; I will guide you with my eye. It is never easy to accept negative criticism but with God all things are possible.

Something beautiful
Something good! God can
make something beautiful
out of every Christian

Act like a child, think like a mature Christian

Nugget # 16: Christians managing "church hurts" in a mature way

The church consists of people who are human beings first and Christians after. The church however serves in different capacities: for edification of the believers, evangelizing, helping, teaching, counseling, correction, nurturing, and building up believers to be mature in Christ.

Within this environment there could be times when Christians encounter misunderstanding, hurtful experiences, misinterpretation of a church rule or Church standards. The term 'Church hurt' can be defined as being wounded due to an unpleasant or misunderstood situation within the church family. The general expectations of a Christian is that they should be kindhearted individuals, loving and caring for each other. The unfortunate thing is sometimes misunderstanding happens or individuals may choose to act out a disobedient behavior for self-gratification. What is helpful when there is a misunderstanding that may cause a hurtful feeling is not to act in the moment if all possible. Take some time to think through what happen, get the facts, get some clarity and get back in the words and let the fruit of the spirit guide the decisions that you will make.

It takes a childlike heart and mind to be ready to forgive those who may cause you some pain. Bear in mind that the church can be viewed as an hospital where individuals can be healed from any and every situation. It is also very important to note that, a church does not consist of perfect people; instead there will be those who will fail, but who are willing to rise up and continue learning how to be better Christians with the help of the Lord.

If you are experiencing any form of church hurts, some tips that can be helpful are:

- Pray about the situations.
- Ask the Lord for the strength to overcome
- Reach out to the individuals whether it is a believer or a leader and talk about the problem.
- Make reference to the words of God when dealing with the matter at hand, (Matthew 18-3-4) and Matthew 18-15
- Never allow a meeting to be confrontational but approach each other with humility of heart and love.
- Forgive -forgiveness is never easy! In fact, I think it's one of the hardest things to do in life but for Christians it should be easy with God's help. Matt 6-15- *"But if you do not forgive men their sins, your Father will not forgive your sins".* Bearing in mind that we hurt the Lord so often with our wrong doings and he forgave us and show his love towards us daily.
- Never wait for long periods of time to deal with a hurt, deal with it as soon as possible.

- Never engaged in gossiping about the name of the believer or believers who may cause a hurt feeling as this can cause more hurt and division within the church. (Psalm 133-1)
- Show love-Paul in 1 Cor.13-4-7describes that "Charity /love suffereth long, and is kind; charity envieth not; charity vaunteth not itself, is not puffed up, 5. Doth not behave itself unseemly, seeketh not her own, is not easily provoked, thinketh no evil; 6. Rejoiceth not in iniquity, but rejoiceth in the truth; 7. Beareth all things, believeth all things, hopeth all things, endureth all things.
- Never disrespect those who watch over your souls (Pastors and other leaders) Heb 13 -17
- Never behave in a disrespectful and rebellious way as this only hurt the soul more.
- Always remember, Christians are human, and can make mistakes. When there is a misunderstanding in church the solutions should not be going from church to church, backsliding, and rebel. Remember there are problems everywhere. It is important to note that whenever the feeling of hurt arises, the spirit of offense will come up in most cases which helps to support the pain and may tempt you to hold on to the hurt in the heart for a longer time. One way to respond to emotional pain of the soul is forgiveness from the heart.
- Why not keep moving forward in your church if the standard matches with the words of God, forgiving and embracing the will of the Father for your life.

- The church is the bride of Christ and the body of Christ is a people set apart to declare God's praises. Even though hard to bear, we shouldn't be surprised when a believer experiences some form of hurt due to a misunderstanding, as Christians it would be less painful if we would see each other as sinners saved by grace and is still working on being better Christians by using God's manual (The Bible).

- When you are experiencing "church hurt", make the decision to talk about the problem. It is helpful to say "You hurt my feelings when you ……………….. It is okay for a Christian to own their feelings, or owning their hurt and be willing to problem solve.

Other scriptures that can be helpful: Ephesians 4-1-6- the primary call here is for Christians to keep the unity in the church. Love covers a multitude of sins (1 Peter 4:8).

When Christians are faced with un-pleasant experiences it could be viewed as a test. God could be testing your faith, your testimony, your character or it could be that the Lord is working something out in your life so that his purposes can be seen. Whenever you are hurt, **<u>just remember</u> that there is a Healer who understands every heartache and pain.** Never allow the experience to turn you away, criticized or rebel. Always remember, Life at best is very brief like the falling of a leaf, so at all times be on the watch!

Hear thy guardian angels say, Thou art in the midst of foes 'watch and pray"

If you would like to see changes or help
someone along the way pick up your pen and
send a word of encouragement today!

Act like a child, think like a mature Christian

Nugget # 17: Christians as an Encourager

Encouragement is essential in the life of a believer and in the church at large. Thus, encouragement should be shared with joy and the hope to lift someone's heart towards the Lord (Col. 4:8).

One of God's desires for His children is for them to encourage each other especially since John 16:33 warned us that in this world we will have trouble. This is pointing Christians to be an encourager to their brethren, their neighbors and the visitors who visit worship service from time to time. Also remember those who are going through troublesome times in their lives. Proverbs 27-17: Iron sharpeneth iron; so a man sharpeneth the countenance of his friend.

When Christians encourage each other, this must be done with a Christ-like heart and with pure motives. In the early church encouragement/exhortation was a daily part of their Christian life. (Acts 13:15)

Hebrew 3:13 reminds Christians that we should encourage/exhort each other until the Lord return. When encouragement is absent from the church, one can feel forgotten, unloved, unimportant, useless, and not a part of the family. Take note that encouragements should be done with believers both locally and internationally.

How can Christians develop the art of being an encourager? Encouragers can be viewed as Ministers of the Lord Jesus Christ and it can be done through these medium:

1. Engaging with each other by using Bible verses or other sources of information as a means to offer encouragement.
2. Use quotes with encouragements
3. Write notes of encouragements
4. Daily devotions
5. Pray one for another
6. Send a text (be respectful when texting)
7. Make a call when possible
8. Send an email (be respectful when emailing)
9. Remember that our Pastors and ministers should be on our list of encouragements.

Christians acting mature with a childlike heart should first pray about being an encourager and also how to encourage each other. Barnabas was nicknamed the son of consolation by the early church (Acts 4:36). He was the kind of Christian you would want to have around today. Barnabas was the type of Christian with a conviction to see the church flourish. Mature Christians should be mindful and exercise wisdom when sending text to their sisters and brothers or to couples. Let the spirit of God guide you as you demonstrate the gift of an encourager.

God knows exactly what you
need and when you need it!

Act like a child, think like a mature Christian

Nugget # 18: Christians honoring their leaders

Pastors and other leaders are ordained to be overseers within the church. Acts 20:28 stated that the Holy Ghost hath made them overseers to feed the church of God. Titus 1:5-9, and 1 Pet. 5:2 are verses that represent facts that pastors or elders represent God's servants with the ability to oversee the day-to-day running of the church.

The role of the leaders can change depending on the situations before them at various times.

- Sometimes a leader maybe gentle, kind and loving and other times there will be the need for reproof and rebuke according to the situations before them (2 Timothy 4-2)
- there maybe the need to meet with a believer about a wrong action displayed (Matthew 18:15–20).
- There will always be the need to point out sin through the words of God to help believers to

honor the Lord and to live righteously in this world. (2 Timothy 3-16)

A Christ like leader will focus on Christ more and less on public approval. (Ephesians 6:6),

Some pointers as to how Christians can honor their leaders: (1 Timothy 5:17)

- Christians should be respectful to their leaders in all situations.
- Christians should affirm their pastors and be obedient to their authority with grace because they keep watch over your souls (Hebrews 13:7)
- Christians should honor their leaders who are following biblical principles so that their work will be a joy and not a burden (Heb. 13:17).
- Christians should pray for their leaders.
- Christians should love their leaders
- Likewise, leaders should love and respect their members as they instruct them in the way of the Lord and be not lords over God's heritage, but being ensamples to the flock. (1Peter 5:3)

Christians should bear in mind that leaders are called by God to take care of the flock which is a enormous and difficult job.

A few questions for reflections:

1. Should Christian be in malice with their leaders?
2. Should Christians speak disrespectful about their leaders?

3. Should Christians go on social media to indirectly send disrespectful messages to vent how they are feeling about a leader or a church?

4. What should a Christian do in regards to a misunderstanding with a leader? A or B ?

a. Have a conversation to talk about the concerns
b. Criticize, blame, quarrel and staying angry

As Christians reflect on these questions, it is encouraged that believers in the Lord Jesus Christ make an effort to behave in such a way that their lives are light bearers so that God is pleased with their words and actions.

God is depending on us under all circumstances to be sober minded and allowing the spirit of God to equip us as to how to behave in our everyday life.

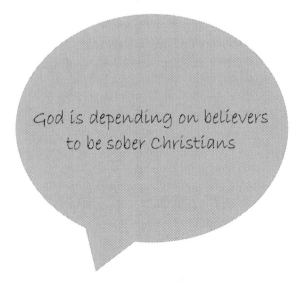

God is depending on believers
to be sober Christians

Nuggets # 19: Christians
letting go of the past

Dwelling in the past can be dangerous for the child of God as this can cause physical, emotional, mental, psychological and spiritual pain. The word of God advises in Isaiah 43:18 "Forget the former things and do not dwell on the past".

There is danger in keeping an unhealthy memory of past hurts and pains. If a memory is affecting the way your relationship is with a brother, sister, spouse or a leader, it is important that the individual who is affected do two things as soon as possible; One is to have a conversation with the individual and secondly, if you are able to let go the hurt and move on with serving the Lord in spirit and in truth that would be a plus of a mature believer, but if you are not able to do so by all means talk about the problem with grace and peace.

Matt 11:28-30 "Come unto me, all ye that labour and are heavy laden, and I will give you rest. Take my yoke upon you, and learn of me;for I am meek and lowly in heart: and ye shall find rest unto your souls. For my yoke is easy, and my burden is light."

Not letting go of past hurts can affect Christians in their homes, in their families, at church, at the work places and in their marriages. This is like a deadly poison for the believers and a concerted effort should be made by all to talk about issues and not holding unto them. Remember the ultimate goal is eternal life and with God all things are possible.

One of the best decisions one can ever make in their life is to let go of what is hurting their hearts and minds.

Act like a child, think like a mature Christian

Nugget # 20: Christians working towards inheriting eternal life

Eternal life is the Christians main goal for living and serving the Lord which make this topic the most important of all. The access of eternal life came to us through the death of Jesus Christ on Calvary cross. Let us therefore come boldly bowing at his feet and confess our sins so that we might be saved. Below are some bible verses that provide the hope of eternal life.

Matt. 19:16-19, stated "And, behold, one came and said unto him, Good Master, what good thing shall I do, that I may have eternal life? And he said unto him, Why callest thou me good? There is none good but one, that is, God: but if thou wilt enter into life, keep the commandments. He saith unto him, which? Jesus said, Thou shalt do no murder, Thou shalt not commit adultery, Thou shalt not steal, Thou shalt not bear false witness. Honor thy father and thy mother: and, Thou shalt love thy neighbor as thyself.

The essence of these verses points Christians to the

importance of obeying the words of the Lord in regards to his commandments in the old and New Testament.

Other commands of the instructions given by Jesus are found in: **(Exodus 20: 1-17)**

In **Matthew 7:21**, Jesus made another important statement: "Not everyone who says to me, 'Lord, Lord,' shall inherit the kingdom of heaven, but he who does the will of My Father in heaven."

This verse clearly speaks to Christians to make every effort to do the will of the Lord and not just to go to church for mere curiosity. It is of great importance that we search the scriptures in a sincere way to truly find out what is the will of God mentioned in Matt.7-21. For Christians to inherit the kingdom there has to be a total change in the way they live their lives.

Additional verses that speaks clearly to Christians as to what is needed to be done to inherit eternal life:

Matthew 5:16

Let your light shine before men in such a way that they may see your good works, and glorify your Father who is in heaven. Shining your light here could be viewed as, the Christian sincerity, faithfulness, courage and their integrity.

Matthew 5:22-24

Therefore if you are presenting your offering at the altar, and there remember that your brother has something against you, leave your offering there before the altar and go; first be reconciled to your brother, and then come and present your offering. This is saying that external act will not do it

Matthew 6:1-4

Beware of practicing your righteousness before men to be noticed by them; otherwise you have no reward with your Father who is in heaven. "So when you give to the poor, do not sound a trumpet before you, as the hypocrites do in the synagogues and in the streets, so that they may be honored by men truly I say to you, they have their reward in full. "But when you give to the poor, do not let your left hand know what your right hand is doing. Never do acts of kindness to show others how rich, or great you are, but out of a heart of love ,care and grace.

Matthew 7:1-29

Do not judge so that you will not be judged. For in the way you judge, you will be judged; and by your standard of measure, it will be measured to you. "Why do you look at the speck that is in your brother's eye, but do not notice the log that is in your own eye?

This verse does not means that Christians should not speak out against sin or wrong doings. What Jesus is warning against is hypocritical, self-righteous judging. It is more of making a spiritual evaluation of the words and behaviors' of wrong doings and not finding fault.

Matthew 18:21-22

Then Peter came and said to Him, "Lord, how often shall my brother sin against me and I forgive him? Up to seven times?" Jesus said to him, "I do not say to you, seven times, but up to seventy times seven. Forgiveness is a difficult thing to do and the lord knows that mankind would need specific instruction to do this act: reflection: if another member of the church sins against you, how often should you forgive?

John 13:34-35

A new commandment I give to you, that you love one another, even as I have loved you, that you also love one another. "By this all men will know that you are my disciples, if you have love for one another."

These verses along with the Ten Commandments in Exodus 20 are important commands that God is expecting his people to obey through faith and grace. The new commandments does not erase the commands that points out the,' thou shall not' How would Christians know what is sin? 1John 3-4 confirms that "sin is the transgressions' of God's laws". The Holy Spirit will help us to overcome sins but as Christians it is a good thing to know what is wrong from right. It's by grace that are we saved. Grace in other words is like getting what we do not deserve from God. Mankind does not deserve forgiveness of our sins, but he gives it to us through Jesus.

Matthew 25:34-46

Then the King will say to those on his right, 'Come, you who are blessed of My Father, inherit the kingdom prepared for you from the foundation of the world. 'For I was hungry, and you gave Me something to eat; I was thirsty, and you gave Me something to drink; I was a stranger, and you invited Me in; naked, and you clothed Me; I was sick, and you visited Me; I was in prison, and you came to Me.

Take note that we will never see Jesus in the flesh but

this is instructing Christians to help others who are in need as we live our lives here on earth.

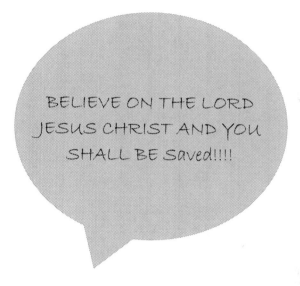

REFLECTION # 1

Congratulations!!! You have completed 20 wonderful nuggets.

A growing or mature Christian is one who is very reflective. They will diagnose, cure and prevent challenges/ problems. The following explains how to apply the DCP method to your life:

Diagnosis: How does the nugget that I have read deal with this issue that I am presently facing?

Cure: Am I applying what is prescribed?

Prevention: How can I use what I have learnt to prevent future occurrences?

Below are brief descriptions of some types of life's challenges that have been discussed throughout this book. As you read through each, stop and reflect. Then ask yourself the following questions:

1. How did I handle the situation **before** reading this book?

2. How am I handling the situation **after** reading the book?

After each reflection, complete the table below. Next, carefully analyse your **before** and **after** responses. If your **after** responses are more favourable than the **before**, YOU HAVE GROWN! However, if they are the same or worse than the before responses, GO BACK TO THE REVELANT NUGGETS AND ALLOW GOD TO RETEACH YOU.

Remember: How you respond is what will make the difference in the life of a Christian!!!

Before	Life's Challenges	After
	• Distresses: which can come in the form of various disappointments in life	
	• Fiery trials: which can be intense encounters and struggles of life	
	• Physical limitations and illnesses: which can leads to dying	
	• Reproach: which can be rejection on account of your faith or holiness	
	• Persecutions: which can come in the form of harassment, discriminations and oppression due to your religious convictions	

	• Fatigue: This can come through the daily pressures of life.	
	• Tribulations: which can come through standing up for the words of the Lord	
	• Temptations: which can come through opportunities that will want you to yield to our sinful nature	
	• Financial experiences	

Pray always pray the
Holy Spirit pleads

REFLECTION # 2

Christians' self-assessments quiz

Take a moment through meditation and devotion and rate yourself as to how are you doing in the Lord and for the Lord. Whatever are your results let it be known to the Lord and seek his guidance as to how to start fulfilling your ministry in his work.

SCALE: **C**-Committed   **A**-Average   **P**-Poor

Questions	C	A	P
Are you feeding your mind on God's word?			
Are you attending church weekly?			
How is your prayer life?			
Do you visit the shut ins, prisoners or the hospitalized?			
Are you on time for worship?			
Are you worshipping the Lord in spirit and truth?			
Are you witnessing to your family and to your neighbors?			
Are you demonstrating a childlike behavior and thinking maturely in the Lord?			

How is your moral conduct?			
Do you fast and pray when there is a need?			
Are you using the gift/talents that God gave you?			
Are you serving with a zeal?			
Are you tithing?			
Are you a giver in the work of the Lord?			
Are you a complainer?			
Are you more encouraging and less gossiping?			
Are you acting like a child and thinking maturely in the Lord?			
Do you love your neighbors as yourself?			
Can you control your anger?			
Are you behaving wisely in every aspect of your life?			
Are you respectful to your leaders?			
Are you helping to move the church forward?			

Are you involved in these Ministries?	Yes	No
• Youth Fellowship		
• Employment Ministry		
• Teaching young believers ministry		
• Music Ministry		
• Prayer Ministry		
• Singing Ministry		
• Men's and Women Ministry		
• Counseling /Training for couples Ministry		

•	Psychoeducation sessions for those who are single and for the elderly		
•	Out- Reach Ministry		
•	Visit the hospitals, prison, shut-ins, infirmaries and witness within our communities ministry		
•	Health and Wellness Ministry		
•	Help ministry		
•	Substance abuse education Ministry		
•	What is your ministry????		

These are some examples of Christian's engagements in the work of the Lord.

Reflection: Work for the night is coming when Christians works no more.

REFLECTION # 3

A step by step procedure that Christians can apply to solve problems in their daily life

When you are faced with any problem try these simple steps:

- First seek the Lord in prayer
- Step 1: Define the Problem that is of concern
- Step 2: Talk about the Problem.
- Step 3: List or discuss possible solutions
- Step 4: Select the best option
- Step 5: Implement the solution agreed on

Problem solving is identifying the root cause of the problem that is of concern and applying a workable solution by implementing a plan of action.

REFLECTION # 4

Bible Verses for Daily Meditations

1. 2 Timothy 3:16-17- All Scripture are written by God and profitable for teaching, for reproof, for correction, and for training in righteousness.

   For meditation: when the words of God offer a rebuke, pray and seek the face of the Lord

2. Col. 3-2- Set your affection on things above, not on things on the earth.
   For **Meditation**: Be deliberate about what your mind is focus on.
3. Colossians 3:1 If you then be risen with Christ, seek those things which are above, …

   For mediation: If we are searching or seeking after something important in life we will go after it which takes time and energy. Searching the scriptures needs the same time and energy to read the words of God for guidance for our lives.

4. 1 Chronicles 22:19 now set your heart and your soul to seek the LORD your God.

5. 1 John 2:15-17 Love not the world, neither the things that are in the world.

6. 2 Corinthians 5:17 -Therefore, if anyone is in Christ, he is a new creation. The old has passed away; behold, the new has come.

7. 1 Peter 5:6- Humble yourselves, therefore, under the mighty hand of God so that at the proper time he may exalt you,

8. Proverbs 10:11 -The mouth of the righteous is a fountain of life, but the mouth of the wicked conceals violence.

9. Psalms 133-1 Behold, how good and how pleasant it is for brethren to dwell together in unity!

10. Hebrews 13-21 Make you perfect in every good work to do his will, working in you that which is well pleasing in his sight, through Jesus Christ, to whom be glory forever and ever. Amen

11. Romans 12:1- I beseech you therefore, brethren, by the mercies of God, that ye present your bodies a living sacrifice, holy, acceptable unto God, which is your reasonable service.

12. Psalms 121- 1-5 I will lift up mine eyes unto the hills, from whence cometh my help. My help cometh from the LORD, which made heaven and earth. He will not suffer thy foot to be moved: he that keepeth thee will now slumber. Behold, he that keepeth Israel shall neither slumber nor sleep. The LORD is thy keeper: the LORD is thy shade upon thy right hand.

13. 1 John 3-2.Beloved, now are we the son of God and it doth not yet appear what we shall be: but we know that, when he shall appear, we shall be like him; for we shall see him as he is.

14. Ephesians 4:1-2 - I therefore, a prisoner for the Lord, urge you to walk in a manner worthy of the calling to which you have been called, with all humility and gentleness, with patience, bearing with one another in love.

There are five basic tools that can assist individuals to cope with difficult situations: Prayer, Reading the bible, Fasting, worship and fellowship with the saints.

WHO WILL THIS BOOK HELP?

Think like a child! Act like a mature Christian offers some profound tips with a spiritual focus to help Christians to consider the importance of taking the time to read the Bible, and meditate on His words. Thus, allowing the words of God to help them to grow in their daily Christian life.

This book can help those:

- ❖ Who are new in serving the Lord
- ❖ Who are worshippers
- ❖ Who are serving the Lord for many years but are not growing maturely in the Lord
- ❖ Who are struggling to stay on the path of righteousness
- ❖ Who wants to be better Christian
- ❖ Who are serious about going to the kingdom of God
- ❖ Who loves the Lord, but fails to honor Him sometimes
- ❖ Who attend church services but are not committed to the cause or to change their life

ABOUT THE AUTHOR

Murween Perry-Rose is a Christian for most of her life and serves as a minister within her church. She finds pleasure and joy in devoting her life to know more about the Lord in order to grow in Him and more importantly to be a mature child of the King. Murween is a wife and mother. She is also a member of the Counseling profession, a Certified Relationship Coach and Motivational Speaker and she is also a Prepare Enrich Facilitator in Pre-Marital and couples counseling. Murween loves people and enjoy serving others in any way she can.

Printed in the United States
by Baker & Taylor Publisher Services